NO REPENTANCE NO FORGIVENESS

GOD LOVES YOU, BUT IS HIS FORGIVENESS UNCONDITIONAL?

BRUCE BROCK

WINEPRESS **WP** PUBLISHING

WinePress Publishing (PO Box 428, Enumclaw, WA 98022) functions only as book publisher. As such, the ultimate design, content, editorial accuracy, and views expressed or implied in this work are those of the author.

Unless otherwise noted, all Scriptures are taken from the New King James Version, © 1979, 1980, 1982 by Thomas Nelson, Inc., Publishers. Used by permission.

Extract taken from Poems by Steve Turner, published by Lion Publishing PLC, 2002. Copyright © 2002 Steve Turner.

ISBN 13: 978-1-57921-905-5
ISBN 10: 1-57921-905-5
Library of Congress Catalog Card Number: 2007924410

TABLE OF CONTENTS

FOREWORD

And forgive us our debts, as we forgive our debtors.

(Matthew 6:12)

We have a responsibility as followers of Jesus to forgive as we have been forgiven. This is a much easier task when we understand what that really means. My husband's book, *No Repentance, No Forgiveness,* will take you a huge step closer to that goal.

—KATHY BROCK

PREFACE

Dear Reader,

First, allow me to thank you for committing your time and attention to read this little book. I pray you will be blessed with a greater understanding of this foundational doctrine of "forgiveness and repentance." These two words are so familiar to all of us that we seldom think about what they actually mean and how they are to be observed in our lives.

Some individuals are in unhealthy relationships because they sincerely believe God has required them to stay. There are some who are being terribly abused and genuinely believe it is God's will to continue and remain open to the abuser. My prayer for those individuals is that they would see the truth of God's love. Our Father loves us and wants the best for us. He is so good and will never tempt us with evil. Would this quality of His fatherhood cause Him to desire to see His children abused (not being persecuted for righteousness' sake) by evil people? What does it mean to turn the other cheek or to go the extra mile?

While I do not pretend to be the last word on this or any other subject, hopefully this book will bring clarity and answers to some of these issues. In fact, it was a comment made by Pastor Willie George shortly after September 11, 2001, that became the inspiration for this book.

I owe a special acknowledgement to my wife, Kathy. The thirty-three years of our marriage are a special gift to me from God. I am thankful for God's favor in putting Kathy and me together.

Thank you to everyone who helped with the rewrite. My daughter, Carolyne, helped so much with finishing the manuscript. She is so patient with her dad. Thanks also to my administrator, Geri, for her help, and to all the wonderful people on staff and in my extended family of Faith Community Church.

Most of all, I owe thanksgiving to my Lord Jesus. I never cease to be amazed at His amazing grace as His plans continue to unfold in my life. While the journey has had lots of ups and downs, I would not take anything for my journey. Thank you, Jesus, for saving me and help me to bring You glory.

May God grant you wisdom and revelation in His Truth as you continue to read this book.

In His love,
Pastor Bruce Brock

CHAPTER ONE

DEFINING OUR TERMS

If you saw something a little different in the Word of God than what you previously believed, would you be willing to change your mind? Since our understanding of Scripture is progressive, our doctrine is growing and being shaped as we study and hear the Word preached. If I see truth in Scripture that differs from what I think, I should change my mind.

As we study, our understanding of Scripture grows (*Sola Scriptura*). In fact, I would love to buy back some of my teaching tapes from a few years ago and destroy them, because I've learned since then. We should all be growing.

Words are the means by which we communicate, yet some of the terms we use can be misleading. Terms such as "unconditional love," "forgiveness," and "free will" can easily be misunderstood. For example, what does unconditional love mean? Do we find that term in Scripture? Does it mean unconditional acceptance? The obvious answer is no. OK then, how does that fit in with the forgiveness we are commanded to extend? Please read this little book through to the end. This will keep you from drawing a wrong conclusion.

Jesus came teaching "the kingdom of heaven is at hand, repent." We say that God's love is unconditional, but there is a condition to receiving His love, and the condition that has to be met is repentance and then faith. People will be judged because they didn't repent and believe. This does not mean that God is not love. In fact, Romans 5:8 says that God proved His love for us "in that while we were still sinners, Christ died for us." We know that "God is love" (1 John 4:8), but Revelation 19:11–21 shows us another side of this issue:

> Now I saw heaven opened, and behold, a white horse. And He who sat on him was called Faithful and True, and in righteousness He judges and makes war. His eyes were like a flame of fire, and on His head were many crowns. He had a name written that no one knew except Himself. He was clothed with a robe dipped in blood, and His name is called The Word of God. [This is a definite reference from John, telling us this is Jesus.] And the armies in heaven, clothed in fine linen, white and clean, followed Him on white horses. Now out of His mouth goes a sharp sword, that with it He should strike the nations. And He Himself will rule them with a rod of iron. He Himself treads the winepress of the fierceness and wrath of Almighty God. And He has on His robe and on His thigh a name written: King of Kings and Lord of Lords. Then I saw an angel standing in the sun; and he cried with a loud voice, saying

to all the birds that fly in the midst of heaven, "Come and gather together for the supper of the great God, that you may eat the flesh of kings, the flesh of captains, the flesh of mighty men, the flesh of horses and of those who sit on them, and the flesh of all people, free and slave, both small and great." And I saw the beast, the king of the earth, and their armies, gathered together to make war against Him who sat on the horse and against His army. Then the beast was captured, and with him the false prophet who works signs in his presence, by which he deceived those who received the mark of the beast and those who worshipped his image. These two were cast alive into the lake of fire burning with brimstone. And the rest were killed with the sword which proceeded from the mouth of Him who sat on the horse. And all the birds were filled with their flesh.

What about Isaiah 6? God is thrice "holy" (the word is given the maximum emphasis in Hebrew). Would you say that God's holiness is seen in His judgment of sinners? Yes, of course we would. One attribute of God, such as love, does not diminish another, such as holiness. This is the same Jesus who said from the cross, "Father, forgive them, for they do not know what they do." I have a question: were they forgiven? Jesus made it plain that the Son of Man has been given authority on Earth to forgive sins, but Jesus' prayer from the cross did not cause them to become regenerate. In my understanding, the only sin forgiven was their sin of crucifying God's Son. If they did not later repent and believe in the Lord Jesus, they were not saved.

Forgiveness and Relationship

We know that as Christians we are commanded to forgive as God in Christ forgave us, with that same measure. Actually, we were forgiven of much more than we could ever forgive somebody else—God forgave us our sin! No relationship can survive without forgiveness. Forgiveness in this context of relationship is what I would like to examine. Here is where we, as Christians, can try to make forgiveness into something it is not. Forgiveness is meant to be a benefit and a blessing in our relationships. The closer the relationship, the more important forgiveness is. "Fellowship" is this dynamic within this close relationship that we have as God's family.

However, what about forgiveness in the context of our enemies? There is no fellowship connected to this kind of forgiveness. What does this look like? Let's read Matthew 18:21–35:

> Then Peter came to Him and said, "Lord, how often shall my brother sin against me ['my brother'—that's the context of a relationship], and I forgive him? Up to seven times?" Jesus said to him, "I do not say to you, up to seven times, but up to seventy times seven. Therefore the kingdom of heaven is like a certain king who wanted to settle accounts with his servants. And when he had begun to settle accounts, one was brought to him who owed him ten thousand talents. But as he was not able to pay, his master commanded that he be sold, with his wife and children and all that he had, and that payment be made. [That was just. He owed the money, so by putting him in debtor's prison, the debt would be paid.] The servant therefore fell down before him,

saying, 'Master, have patience with me, and I will pay you all.' Then the master of that servant was moved with compassion, released him, and forgave him the debt. [This debt was an astronomical sum of money—millions and millions of dollars.] But that servant went out and found one of his fellow servants who owed him a hundred denarii [a denarius was one day's wage for a laboring man]; and he laid hands on him and took him by the throat, saying, 'Pay me what you owe!' So his fellow servant fell down at his feet and begged him, saying, 'Have patience with me, and I will pay you all.' [These are the same words and actions he used with the master.] And he would not, but went and threw him into prison till he should pay the debt. So when his fellow servants saw what had been done, they were very grieved, and came and told their master all that had been done. Then his master, after he had called him, said to him, 'You wicked servant! I forgave you all that debt because you begged me. Should you not also have had compassion on your fellow servant, just as I had pity on you?' And his master was angry, and delivered him to the torturers until he should pay all that was due to him. So My heavenly Father also will do to you if each of you, from his heart, does not forgive his brother his trespasses."

This teaching on forgiveness is in the context of community. This is not in the context of the evil of the world coming against you. You need to make that distinction. This is very important. Jesus is teaching us to forgive because we've been forgiven, but there are many lessons we could draw from this. The one I want to focus on is this: how forgiveness was offered. It wasn't offered until the servant asked for mercy. Forgiveness was not offered until the servant asked for mercy, and when he did, then he was forgiven by the master.

To Repent or Not Repent

I've always believed and taught that we need to forgive people whether they repent or not; this may not be entirely true. This may be difficult for you, but hang with me and follow this closely. I did not say you should hate the offender or become embittered toward them or be mean-spirited to them. (Vengeance still belongs to the Lord.) A problem we might have is the wrong definition of what forgiveness is. Remember forgiveness in the context of relationship, and the benefit of relationship is fellowship.

Jesus came preaching that the kingdom of heaven is at hand and to repent (Matthew 4:17). He did not preach unqualified forgiveness and acceptance. You don't get mercy from God until you repent and believe. No repentance, no forgiveness. It's absolutely true.

So, let's talk about unconditional love. What is unconditional love? If there is a condition to receiving salvation, which is repentance and faith, is unconditional love blanket forgiveness? No. Is unconditional love blanket pardon? No. Does it mean unconditional acceptance of behavior? Obviously not. If we are going to use the term "unconditional love," we better know what we are saying. We can't tell the world that God has unconditional love for them because that is not the truth. They hear "blanket forgiveness, blanket acceptance of behavior," and that is not what God said. To me, God's love is the fact that God loves me when I don't deserve love but when I deserve justice. However, because of God's grace, I repented and received the free gift of salvation; but if we don't repent—no salvation, no forgiveness. Do not pass go, no two hundred bucks, no "get out of jail free" card! In that case, no "get out of hell free" card! There is no such thing.

Even after salvation, God does not just "blanketly" accept our behavior. The Bible is very clear that He disciplines His children. I have two girls, and when they were little we spanked them when it was needed. I believe that's the way to raise children. We didn't delight in spanking them. It wasn't some kind of morbid pleasure that we had. We didn't abuse them. We very carefully disciplined them. But my love for them was the same when I was spanking them as when we were opening Christmas presents. What was the purpose of spanking? Put very simply, to bring them to repentance. Now here is where we have gone wrong as the Church. We haven't understood that there is a difference between love and forgiveness. God loves the world, but those who don't repent are not forgiven. This is called common grace. All share in God's *common* grace, but only those who repent and believe share in God's *saving* grace. In order for people to receive forgiveness, there must be repentance.

Look at Luke 17:1–3. This was an eye-opener for me. Jesus said to His disciples:

> "It is impossible that no offenses should come, but woe to him through whom they do come! It would be better for him if a millstone were hung around his neck, and he were thrown into the sea, than that he should offend one of these little ones. Take heed to yourselves. If your brother sins against you, rebuke him . . ."

Notice He says if your brother sins against you. It's not about him taking your parking spot or that you didn't get invited to the party. The context is a major offense. Something you know shouldn't be done again and something that, if he is made aware of, he knows it shouldn't be done again. So notice what Jesus says, "If your brother sins against you, rebuke him; and if he repents, forgive him." (Interesting, "and if he repents, forgive him.") Verse 4:

> "And if he sins against you seven times in a day,
> and seven times in a day returns to you, saying,
> 'I repent,' you shall forgive him."

We know that if he comes and says he repents, we are to forgive him. That's a no-brainer. This also gives us some illustration on repentance. Repentance means changing direction or changing your mind. Unfortunately, even with genuine repentance the sin may show up again.

Hebrews 12:1 tells us that as Christians we have sins that easily beset us. If I believe repentance means I have changed and that particular sin will no longer beset me, I am set up for some problems. What happens when that sin causes me to stumble again? Did I really repent or not? On these occasions the devil (who loves to accuse me and you) heaps condemnation on my head telling me all kinds of lies about how God feels about me and how rotten I am.

Look closer at this passage in Luke 17. Jesus said seven times, same offense, and probably the same day; yet if he turns and says, "I repent," he is to be forgiven. This shows us how God forgives us. When I go to God and confess, "Father, I can't believe it! I did it again and I need Your strength to help," He forgives me. There is no question of lordship; therefore, I will not run from Him, but I choose to run to Him when I fail. My heart is contrite and repentant. He understands that I am dust, and He loves me because I am His child.

Now notice Luke 17:3: "if he repents, forgive him." Most of us do not tell our brother when he sins against us. Is it because we have been infected with political correctness, or are we just cowards? Ephesians 4:15 tells us to grow up and speak the truth to each other in love. But instead we say to ourselves, "I won't say anything, but I will forgive him." There are several problems with this approach. First of all, we are condoning improper behavior, and second, we are not following scriptural guidelines. Can the relationship truly be repaired like this? Forgiveness as Jesus taught in Luke 17 is in the context of relationship, and the benefit of relationship is fellowship.

Tolerance

Christian love is not unconditional acceptance. In America, we have freedom of religion. I will not infringe upon your right to worship whomever or whatever you want. That's fine. I won't infringe upon your right to worship a chair, but I will tell you that it won't do any good. All religions aren't created equal. There is a great distinction between Jesus and Mohammed or Jesus and Buddha. Some would call me intolerant, but truth is truth. Truth is not truth because someone genuinely believes it. Truth will not compromise and it will not bend. The truth is not that I am intolerant—you can worship whomever you choose—but it is my responsibility to stand up and tell you the truth of God's Word. I will not be politically correct and neither should you. Tolerance is the attitude that as long as it doesn't hurt anybody, and if you really believe it, it's OK. It is not OK! Hell will be full of sincere people. In fact, the Bible says that if I don't warn you, and you go there, your blood is on my hands. I don't want that.

Look at Steve Turner's satirical poem on tolerance entitled "Creed":

> We believe in Marxfreudanddarwin.
> We believe everything is OK as long as you
> don't hurt anyone to the best of your definition
> of hurt, and to the best of your knowledge.

We believe in sex before, during, and after marriage.
We believe in the therapy of sin.
We believe that adultery is fun.
We believe that sodomy's OK.
We believe that taboos are taboo.

We believe that everything's getting better despite evidence to the contrary.
The evidence must be investigated.
You can prove anything with evidence.

We believe there's something in horoscopes, UFO's, and bent spoons.
Jesus was a good man just like Buddha, Mohammed, and ourselves.
He was a good moral teacher although we think His good morals were bad.

We believe that all religions are basically the same—at least the one that we read was.
They all believe in love and goodness.
They only differ on matters of creation, sin, heaven, hell, God, and salvation.

We believe that after death comes the Nothing because when you ask the dead what happens they say nothing.
If death is not the end, if the dead have lied, then it's compulsory heaven for all excepting perhaps Hitler, Stalin, and Genghis Khan.

We believe in Masters and Johnson.
What's selected is average.

What's average is normal.
What's normal is good.

We believe in total disarmament.
We believe there are direct links between warfare and bloodshed.
Americans should beat their guns into tractors and the Russians would be sure to follow.

We believe that man is essentially good.
It's only his behavior that lets him down.
This is the fault of society.
Society is the fault of conditions.
Conditions are the fault of society.

We believe that each man must find the truth that is right for him.
Reality will adapt accordingly.
The universe will readjust.
History will alter.
We believe that there is no absolute truth excepting the truth that there is no absolute truth . . .

Can you see the ridiculousness of this attitude of tolerance? Everything is *not* fine. Not to us and certainly not to God. The world wants a God without wrath who took man without sin into a kingdom without justice through the ministrations of a Christ without the cross. The cross is the greatest display of God's love. There is no doubt about it. But the cross is also the greatest display of God's justice. Don't forget that. The cross was not an option. It was not an elective. The cross of Christ not only illustrates God's love but also illustrates how seriously God looks at sin.

We have been very sloppy on this issue of forgiveness. "I forgive you. Go ahead and just do it." Let me give you an example to illustrate my point before I develop it any further. How many women today are living in abusive marriages? They are somebody's punching bag because the Church told them, "Well, you know divorce is a sin. You have to forgive him. God's grace will cover you." Let me tell you something. That's a bunch of bunk! The Bible calls no woman to live in a relationship where she is somebody's punching bag. And any man that's cowardly enough to beat on a woman doesn't deserve to have a woman. Cultures in our world that advocate this kind of treatment are disdained—and they should be. But the Church has said, "Forgive him." Remember what we just learned from Scripture: without repentance there is no forgiveness. Does that mean she doesn't love him? I didn't say that. Does that mean she is mean-spirited? I didn't say that. Does that mean she's hateful? I didn't say that. She can love him, *but* no repentance, no forgiveness.

Forgiveness Does Not Equal Love

Let me give you another extreme example. Let's say that you were sexually molested as a child by a family member. Now you are an adult and have children of your own. Does this mean that you expose your children to this molester? The Church would say, "We have to forgive him," but I would add some qualifiers or conditions. Forgiveness can be extended from the heart, but without repentance on the part of the abuser, there should not be restoration of relationship. Love, yes, but not to open the door for further abuse. John the Baptist preached that "fruit of repentance" must be brought forth to escape God's wrath.

What happens with people (evil people, wife beaters, child molesters, etc.) who know the Church teaches that we have to forgive them unconditionally? They will use it and say, "You're a Christian. You have to forgive me." Look at the context of 2 Corinthians 2:5–7 where there was a man who was put out of the fellowship because of his sin.

> But if anyone has caused grief, he has not grieved me, but all of you to some extent—not to be too severe. This punishment [being put out of the fellowship] which was inflicted by the majority is sufficient for such a man, so that, on the contrary, you ought rather to forgive and comfort him, lest perhaps such a one be swallowed up with too much sorrow.

Sorrow indicates repentance had come. So because repentance has come, Paul says now forgive him. Verse 8: "Therefore I urge you to reaffirm your love to him." Love was always there but forgiveness wasn't. When repentance came, forgiveness was forthcoming, but all the time love was there. However, there was no relationship or the benefit of relationship (which is fellowship) as long as there was no repentance. This is very liberating!

Let's look at the story of the prodigal son in Luke 15, beginning in verse 11. We know the story. The son demanded his inheritance and the father gave it to him. He goes off to a far country where he lives like the devil, spends all his money on prostitutes and partying, and finally runs out of money. He's broke, so he hires himself out to a pig farmer to take care of the pigs. One day he is feeding the pigs and realizes the pigs are eating better than he is! He says, "You know, I'm going back to my dad's house. At least I can be a servant there and have food." So he goes back to his father's house. The father sees him coming and runs to meet him. The father begins to hug him, and the son says, "Dad, I just want to be a hired hand." The father says,

"I won't hear of that. No, you're my son, who was dead, and now you've come back. Here's the robe, here's the ring, let's kill the fatted calf and have a party." What do we see here? We see full restoration, full forgiveness, full fellowship and benefits of relationship—but not until he repented. He left the prodigal life and came under his father's authority. Now this is where a lot of us make mistakes in the Church. We tell wayward sons, wayward friends, and wayward believers, "That's OK. I forgive you." Notice that the father didn't call his son at the pig farm and say, "Do you need some more money for that hooker this weekend? How you doing on whiskey? I'll send you $500. OK, I love you, son. God bless. I'm praying for you." That didn't happen! Do you see it? No repentance, no forgiveness, because when forgiveness comes, the fruit of the relationship is restored, which is fellowship, and everything that goes with it.

What do we do when we continue to maintain fellowship when the sin is there? We condone the wrong behavior. "Ah, Pastor, that's a hard message. You're not walking in love, Pastor." Did you know that if you lived your life like Jesus lived His, ninety percent of Christians would accuse you of not walking in love? That's a generalization, but read the Gospels, where Jesus called them "brood of vipers, spawn of serpents." That doesn't sound like love to me, does it to you? Why? Because, once again, without repentance there is no forgiveness. Jesus was not meek and mild when He drove out the money changers.

Look at 1 Corinthians 5, verses 9 and 10. Paul says,

> I wrote to you in my epistle not to keep company with sexually immoral people. Yet I certainly did not mean with the sexually immoral people of this world, or with the covetous, or extortioners, or idolaters, since then you would need to go out of the world.

In other words, you'd have to go live in a monastery some place not to be exposed to people of the world. But he clarifies this. Verse 11: "But now I have written to you not to keep company with anyone named a brother, who is sexually immoral, or covetous, or an idolater, or a reviler, or a drunkard, or an extortioner—not even to eat with such a person." What's the issue? When that sin comes in, you are to withdraw fellowship with anyone named a brother. Why? Because you can't extend forgiveness and the fruit of relationship, which is fellowship, until there is repentance. This is where the Church has fallen down on the job big time; we're not training people. Instead we coddle people and, as a result, people aren't being disciplined. Love expresses correction because of love itself.

God-ordained Institutions

Now I want to look at this on a different level. We've talked about it on the level of the Church. Let's bring it up to a national level or to a cultural level. God has ordained certain institutions in the earth. The first one is at home. We know that the first home was in the Garden of Eden. God instituted the home, first, to illustrate that He is a father. The relationships we have as husband and wife and children typifies and exemplifies the relationship God wants to have with His people.

God also instituted the Church. He ordained the Church in the earth, and the purpose of the Church in the earth is to bring the ministry and the Word of reconciliation to the lost—to shine the light, to be the salt, and to advance the kingdom. The Church is to glorify God.

Third, God also instituted government in the earth—just as much as the family and just as much as the Church. We'll see this in Genesis chapter nine, verses 1 and 2. (Now I'm going to get very politically incorrect!)

> So God blessed Noah and his sons [they had just come out of the ark; the flood is over], and said to them: "Be fruitful and multiply, and fill the earth. And the fear of you and the dread of you shall be on every beast of the earth, on every bird of the air, on all that move on the earth, and on all the fish of the sea. They are given into your hand."

In other words, the animals will no longer come to you like they did in the ark; now you'll have to go after them. Verse 3: "Every moving thing that lives shall be food for you . . ." How about that? Pork ribs, barbecue, Mexican food, cheeseburgers! Isn't that good news? If you're a vegetarian, that's OK, but I'm not. Verse 3 continues: "I have given you all things, even as the green herbs." Verses 4–6:

> "But you shall not eat flesh with its life, that is, its blood. Surely for your lifeblood I will demand a reckoning; from the hand of every beast I will require it, and from the hand of man. From the hand of every man's brother I will require the life of man. Whoever sheds man's blood, by man his blood shall be shed; for in the image of God He made man . . ."

Civil Law

So, God ordained human government, and the next thing He did was institute capital punishment. Can you believe it? What about the people who carry signs outside prisons when someone is going to be executed that read: "Thou shalt not kill! Thou shalt not kill!" Well, it may say that in the King James Version, but it's actually not an accurate rendering of the

Hebrew text. It really is, "Thou shalt not do murder." If God commanded, "Thou shalt not kill," He violated His own commandment. Didn't He empower David to kill Goliath? The command is, "Thou shalt not do murder." Some of those people carrying signs should have written underneath that: "Nor do I read my Bible."

Allow me, please, to be political for a moment. People criticize the deterrence of capital punishment. In my opinion, it's not a deterrent because we have become so wrong-headed. By the time all the appeals are exhausted along with everything else, so much time has passed that the victims have been forgotten, and the seriousness of the crime has faded from memory. It's like Dad taking Junior into the bedroom to administer a spanking and Mom says, "Oh, no, I can't stand it when you spank him. It just breaks my heart!" Hey, Dad may take him in there and bend him over and wear him out, but that spanking is only fifty percent effective because Junior knows Mom is not for it. I think that's the problem in America today. So many people are against criminal punishment and they are crying out with a loud voice. If we would, with one voice, demand an end to the shedding of innocent blood and that justice be brought to those that do, then it would be a deterrent like God intended. Life is sacred! Man is made in the image of God and evil people must be dealt with, including terrorists, murderers, and the like. Human life is sacred.

God did not ordain the Church to carry out civil law. Faith Community Church is not going to hire someone to drop bombs on terrorists in Afghanistan. This is not our job. We are the Church, and our assignment is to preach the gospel and be the salt and light to the world. However, I'll be glad to pray that bombs hit their intended target! Murder and terrorism should be punished, and God is all for that. People worry about innocent casualties during these conflicts and ask, "Are we not responsible for this innocent blood?" We are not responsible if we have integrity in the conflict, because this innocent blood is on the hands of the terrorists—not us. It really is that simple. God *hates* feet that are swift to shed innocent blood (Proverbs 1:16).

Some people have become so confused about justice that this is what they believe: If somebody breaks into my home to burgle my house and to abuse my family, I will not resist. So what am I supposed to do, make him a sandwich? If somebody breaks into my house, I will defend my family. Yet here is where we have made the mistake. Yes, the Bible says, "whoever slaps you on your right cheek, turn the other to him also" (Matthew 5:39), but that is in the context of being persecuted for your faith. If you are going to go the extra mile, it's in the context of being persecuted for your faith. If somebody beats me up for preaching the gospel, I am not going to retaliate. I am not going to get a couple of big guys and go beat the snot out of the guy. If I get beat up for preaching the gospel, I'll rejoice because I've got rewards in Heaven. On the other hand, if somebody tries to come into my house and mess with my wife and my kids, they've got Smith & Wesson to deal with, and I see no conflict between the two situations. This really offends some people, but I believe Scripture supports this view.

In Romans 12:18–21, the apostle Paul says, "If it is possible, as much as depends on you, live peaceably with all men" (verse 18). Let's talk about international conflict and use the nation of Israel and their enemies that surround them. For years people have tried to broker various peace accords without lasting results. Israel has offered great compromises yet the terrorism continues. Should we expect Israel to ignore the terrorists while their innocent civilians are being slaughtered? The United States would not tolerate these kinds of atrocities.

Verse 19: "Beloved (speaking to Christians), do not avenge yourselves . . ." Some Christians would say, "We must be careful that we do not attack the terrorists in a spirit of vengeance."

What kind of attitude would you carry in this conflict? Should we write "John 3:16" on the bombs? That's not what Paul is saying here. Read what he says: "do not avenge yourselves, but rather give place to wrath . . ." In other words, "Get out of the way and let God's wrath come." Verse 19 continues: "for it is written, 'Vengeance is mine, I will repay,' says the Lord." Verses 20 and 21:

> "Therefore if your enemy is hungry, feed him; if he is thirsty, give him a drink; for in so doing you will heap coals of fire on his head." Do not be overcome by evil, but overcome evil with good.

Continuing into the next chapter (the Epistles were not originally written in chapter and verse), he is still talking about the same thing. Verses 1–4a:

> Let every soul be subject to the governing authorities. For there is no authority except from God, and the authorities that exist are appointed by God. Therefore whoever resists the authority resists the ordinance of God, and those who resist will bring judgment on themselves. For rulers are not a terror to good works, but to evil. Do you want to be unafraid of the authority? Do what is good, and you will have praise from the same. For he [the authority] is God's minister to you for good. But if you do evil, be afraid; [now notice this] for he does not bear the sword in vain; for he is God's minister . . .

How do you give place to wrath, as we read in chapter twelve? Paul shows us right here: it is governmental authority.

In wartime, it would be the armed forces. In a nation during peacetime, it would be the civil authorities. Verses 4b–6:

> . . . an avenger to execute wrath on him who practices evil. Therefore you must be subject, not only because of wrath but also for conscience' sake. For because of this you also pay taxes [thank God], for they are God's ministers attending continually to this very thing.

Let's go a bit further. Once again, we do not defend ourselves when it comes to persecution for the faith. We turn the other cheek. We go the extra mile. We return good for evil.

Look at Matthew 26 and see what happened in the Garden of Gethsemane when Judas came and betrayed Jesus. We know Peter takes his sword out, cuts off Malchus' ear, Jesus puts the ear back on, and then says to Peter in verse 52, "Put your sword in its place, for all who take the sword will perish by the sword." We quote that verse and say, "Well, there it is, Pastor, you shouldn't have a sword." Now, let's look at it in context. Jesus is about to endure the persecution of the cross. For this very reason He came. He is not saying, "Don't defend Me." He is saying in this case to put the sword away because it's not appropriate. Look at the next verse. He illustrates that even further. He says in verse 53, "Or do you not think that I cannot now pray to My Father, and He will provide Me with more than twelve legions of angels?" In other words, "Peter, I don't need you to defend Me now. For this purpose I came."

But now go to Luke's gospel, chapter 22 (verse 36): "Then He (Jesus) said to them . . ." Once again Jesus is on the way to Gethsemane (verse 39), so we are in the stage of Jesus' ministry when He is preparing to go to the cross. He said to them in verse 36: "But now, he who has a money bag, let him take it, and likewise a knapsack; and he who has no sword [talking to

His disciples], let him sell his garment and buy one." Jesus is not making a fashion statement: "That just doesn't look right without the sword"! What's He saying here? He is telling the disciples that they may need to be able to defend themselves, so buy a sword.

I want to exhort you for a minute. It is not wrong to want to see wicked people punished. Granted, there is no joy in it; we don't relish it. God Himself said that His soul has no pleasure in the death of the wicked. But even so, that doesn't deter His justice. In Matthew 23:23, Jesus spoke to the scribes and Pharisees and said, "Woe to you, scribes and Pharisees, hypocrites! For you pay tithe of mint and anise and cumin, and have neglected the weightier matters of the law: justice and mercy and faith . . ."

Justice

We preach a lot about faith. We preach a lot about mercy. I think we haven't preached enough about justice. God is a God of justice. Societies with radical world views who teach their children to hate and murder the innocent are under God's curse. They have put themselves in place for God's wrath and judgment. I don't think there is any way you can dispute that. In Genesis 9:5–6, God lets us know what He thinks of the sacredness of life. We are made in the image of God, and for someone to willfully take another's life requires retribution by the "government" God has instituted in the earth. We are called to live at peace with our fellow men as much as is possible. When that becomes impossible, justice must prevail. We, the Church, must not take the law into our own hands but rather pray and support our leaders so that God's plan will come to pass.

So remember, when we talk about forgiveness, let's think about what we are saying. When we say we forgive, are we extending the benefit of relationship, which is fellowship and everything that goes along with it, to someone who is unrepentant? We are commanded to love them, but we are also commanded to be circumspect and prudent.

TWO SIDES TO FORGIVENESS

Perhaps I have struck a nerve with this message of forgiveness. For example, if you are a woman in an abusive relationship, you should be relieved to know that God has not called you to remain in a relationship where you are somebody's punching bag. The Church has told us in the past that we have to stay in there, we have to forgive, etcetera; but to illustrate, try to see forgiveness as a $100 bill. If you go to the bank with a $100 bill and all you have on it is a picture of Benjamin Franklin and nothing on the back (which happens to be Independence Hall), it is not legal tender. You can go to the bank with hundreds of $100 bills with only one side printed, but they are not acceptable as legal tender because they have to have something on the back.

We should allow the Word to frame our understanding as to what forgiveness is and is not in the context of relationship.

One Side of the Bill

Ephesians 4:32 says, "And be kind to one another, tender-hearted, forgiving one another, even as God in Christ forgave you." Paul was talking to the community of believers. When He forgave you, He discharged all debt and all penalties. Would you say that when He forgave you He completely forgave you? The answer to all of these is yes! But can you say that when He forgave you, He forgave you unconditionally? No. He did not forgive us unconditionally. The condition to God forgiving us was our acceptance of Christ alone for salvation. If I don't accept Jesus, even though God's forgiveness has been offered to those who would believe, that's only half of the $100 bill. The other half of the $100 bill is my looking to Christ and putting my faith in Him. Now I have the $100 bill that's legal tender as far as heaven is concerned. I'm forgiven, and I'm a child of God.

Little Ones

Matthew 18, verses 1–7:

> At that time the disciples came to Jesus, saying, "Who then is greatest in the kingdom of heaven?" Then Jesus called a little child to Him, set him in the midst of them, and said, "Assuredly, I say to you, unless you are converted and become as little children, you will by no means enter the kingdom of heaven. Therefore whoever humbles himself as this little child is the greatest in the kingdom of heaven. Whoever receives one little child like this in My name receives Me. But whoever causes one of these little ones who believe in Me to sin, it would be better for him if a millstone were hung around

> his neck, and he were drowned in the depth of
> the sea. Woe to the world because of offenses!
> For offenses must come, but woe to that man
> by whom the offense comes!"

Now, Jesus is not talking about the guy ahead of you in line who takes two desserts and leaves you none. What He is talking about is that offenses are the things that cause the little ones to sin. Offenses are the things that cause the little ones to fall away. It is not somebody that's taken my parking space. If somebody gets my parking place and I lose the victory over that, boy, great is my faith! Jesus is talking about offenses of such magnitude that they would cause somebody not only to be offended but to stumble and fall from their faith.

So, Jesus continues in verses 8–9:

> If your hand or foot causes you to sin, cut it off
> and cast it from you. It is better for you to enter
> into life lame or maimed, rather than having
> two hands or two feet, to be cast into the ever-
> lasting fire. And if your eye causes you to sin,
> pluck it out . . .

Once again, this is in the context of causing a little one to fall. So, if your hand, foot, or eye causes a little one to fall, better for you to be maimed and not cause a little one to fall than to go through life whole and have this laid to your account.

In verses 10–14, we have the parable of the lost sheep, and Jesus is still talking about the little ones. He says the shepherd would leave the ninety-nine in search of the one who is lost. When he finds the one, he rejoices because he's found the one that was lost.

"Even so it is not the will of the Father who is in heaven that one of these little ones should perish. Moreover if your brother sins against you, go and tell him his fault between you and him alone . . ."

That's difficult, isn't it? Most of us are cowards when it comes to doing this.

Verses 15–17 continue:

"If he hears you, you have gained your brother. But if he will not hear, take with you one or two more, that 'by the mouth of two or three witnesses every word may be established.' And if he refuses to hear them, tell it to the church. But if he refuses even to hear the church, let him be to you like a heathen and a tax collector."

Did He say to hate him? No. What did He say? He said turn him out from the fellowship; no longer extend to him the benefits of community. Why? He's causing little ones to fall away, and even though he's been confronted by his brother, his brother and the friend, and finally the whole flock, because he is unrepentant, he is to be turned out.

Heavenly Authority

Matthew 18:18: "Assuredly, I say to you, whatever you bind on earth will be bound in heaven, and whatever you loose on earth will be loosed in heaven." We've used that verse many times out of context. It is also used in Matthew 16 and is the same application. Church government. Here's what the Lord is saying: when the Church has confronted the offender and the offender has not repented, the Church has heavenly authority to turn the offender out or to bind him from the fellowship. In other words, it says that whatever you bind on earth is what's already bound in heaven, and what you loose on earth is what has already been loosed in heaven. We are not initiating; we are following what heaven initiated. Let me tell you why. Heaven knows the heart of this brother who offends the little one and then is confronted again and again and again but does not repent. Heaven is already active to shut the door. The offender's heart is being revealed to us through this process, and we are merely following what heaven has already done. We have the power by following this procedure to bind him from the fellowship or to loose him and bring him back in. But, once again, we're merely following what heaven has already done. I know we quote this verse a lot and use it out of context, but it is used in relationship to church government.

Verses 19 and 20:

> "Again I say to you that if two of you agree on earth concerning anything that they ask, it will be done for them by My Father in heaven. [Same principle there.] For where two or three are gathered together in My name, I am there in the midst of them."

Here is another verse that we take out of context, but Jesus is saying that when you turn the offender out, He is there with you. You are merely following His authority, and He is there to enforce it.

Then in verses 21–35, Peter came to Jesus and said:

> "Lord, how often shall my brother sin against me, and I forgive him? Up to seven times?" [Peter may be looking for an excuse or perhaps he

was feeling extra "spiritual."] Jesus said to him, "I do not say to you, up to seven times, but up to seventy times seven. Therefore the kingdom of heaven is like a certain king who wanted to settle accounts with his servants. And when he had begun to settle accounts, one was brought to him who owed him ten thousand talents. But as he was not able to pay, his master commanded that he be sold, with his wife and children and all that he had, and that payment be made. The servant therefore fell down before him, saying, 'Master, have patience with me, and I will pay you all.' Then the master of that servant was moved with compassion, released him, and forgave him the debt. [Remember this was a huge sum of money.] But that servant went out and found one of his fellow servants who owed him a hundred denarii; and he laid hands on him and took him by the throat, saying, 'Pay me what you owe!' So his fellow servant fell down at his feet and begged him, saying, 'Have patience with me, and I will pay you all.' And he would not, but went and threw him into prison till he should pay the debt. So when his fellow servants saw what had been done, they were very grieved, and came and told their master all that had been done. Then his master, after he had called him, said to him, 'You wicked servant! I forgave you all that debt because you begged me. [He was mucho teed-off!] Should you not also have had compassion on your fellow servant, just as I had pity on you?' And his master was angry, and delivered him to the torturers until he should pay all that was due to him. [The master reinstated the debt against him and threw his family and him into debtor's prison.] So My heavenly Father also will do to you if each of you, from his heart, does not forgive his brother his trespasses."

We see a lot of truths in that passage about forgiveness. Forgiveness is to be given in infinite measure. We don't count to seven and then kill the guy—maybe this was Peter's thinking. The Lord is telling us here it doesn't matter how many times we forgive him, but notice the context of how forgiveness was given—the servant asked for it. He fell down at the master's feet and asked for mercy.

Now let's go to Luke 17. Once again, forgiveness (the second half of that $100 bill) is extended when repentance comes. This is review, but I think we need to repeat some of these things just for the sake of clarity. In Luke 17:1–3, Jesus said to the disciples,

> "It is impossible that no offenses should come, but woe to him through whom they do come! It would be better for him if a millstone were hung around his neck, and he were thrown into the sea, than that he should offend one of these little ones. Take heed to yourselves. If your brother sins against you [once again, not taking your parking spot or your dessert], rebuke him . . ."

It's hard for us to rebuke our brother who sins against us, because our attitude is either to just forget it or, "Let me at him!" I remember a man a few years ago that took it upon himself to be my abuser. He would call and heap abuse upon me, and I felt obligated to take his calls. I thought I had to forgive him.

In other words, I should extend that $100 bill to him on both sides even though he was just calling me to tell me what a rotten pastor I was. But while listening to his tirades, many times I would lose it on the phone. I would get mad, and then I would have to go to my prayer closet and repent and say, "God, forgive me for losing it. Give me the grace, Lord." If the guy had been in my office, we might have come to blows, and we know God has not called us to that.

Speak the Truth in Love

In fact, let's look at this a little closer: "Rebuke him," Jesus says. In Ephesians 4:14–15, it says:

> . . . that we should no longer be children, tossed to and fro and carried about with every wind of doctrine, by the trickery of men, in the cunning craftiness of deceitful plotting, but, speaking the truth in love, may grow up in all things into Him who is the head—Christ . . .

Speaking the truth in love; that calls for maturity. I'm not there yet, but I'm growing and maturing. How about you? Jesus said if our brother sins against us we are to rebuke him. That doesn't mean that we love to speak the truth, because if all we do is blow up at him, then all we did was manifest an outburst of wrath. But we can communicate the nature of the offense, loving him because God loves him. Since Jesus said we are to do it, then we can, and He will help us!

Look at 2 Thessalonians, chapter 3. Some Christians read this and think it's so hard, "Aren't we just supposed to love everybody?" Yes, we are supposed to love everybody, but that doesn't mean we're supposed to fellowship with everybody.

> But we command you, brethren [in other words, we do more than just strongly suggest], in the name of our Lord Jesus Christ, that you withdraw from every brother who walks disorderly and not according to the tradition which he received from us. . . . And if anyone does not obey our word in this epistle, note that person and do not keep company with him, that he may be ashamed. Yet do not count him as an enemy, but admonish him as a brother.

Here's the balance. You continue to love him but admonish or warn him as a brother. If the offender is never told of the offense, how is he going to know what he is doing wrong?

That's one of the problems with the Church today when compared with the early church. In those days, if somebody was turned out of the church, they couldn't go to the next church down the road and start over again with no history. Today you could offend everybody in your church congregation and then go right down the street and start all over again. There is no accountability. But that doesn't take away the reality of what the Lord is trying to teach us in Scripture. Rebuke him, warn him, and speak the truth in love.

This concept is not an uncommon theme in the New Testament, but I want to show it to you again in Titus 3:10–11:

> Reject a divisive man after the first and second admonition, knowing that such a person is warped and sinning, being self-condemned.

Once again, if a person has been warned twice and he is divisive, reject him, and turn him out from the fellowship. Why would God be so serious and so concerned about these kinds of individuals that He would actually instruct us as the Church to disfellowship them? Because they cause damage; they cause the little ones to fall away. The Bible says a little leaven leavens the whole lump. If you are in a church where mass confusion is allowed to reign, no one is going to grow or be discipled. In fact, people with good sense will leave that church. God is a God of order and government.

Proverbs 6:16–19:

> These six things the Lord hates [that's a very strong term], yes seven are an abomination to Him: A proud look, a lying tongue, hands that shed innocent blood, a heart that devises wicked plans, feet that are swift in running to evil, a false witness who speaks lies, and one who sows discord among brethren.

Mustard Seed Faith

Now go back to Luke 17:3, and let's finish that passage. Jesus says beginning in verse 3, "Take heed to yourselves. If your brother sins against you, rebuke him: and if he repents, forgive him." Give him the other side of the $100 bill. In other words, now you have legal tender to restore fellowship. Verse 4: "And if he sins against you seven times in a day, and seven times in a day returns to you, saying, 'I repent,' you shall forgive him." That's pretty tough. If someone sins against me seven times in one day and seven times that day comes to me and says, "I don't know what's wrong with me. I'm sorry. I blew it again. Please forgive me," what am I supposed to do? Jesus commands me to forgive him. Jesus is saying we are to forgive as God forgave us—it's unlimited.

So you can understand the apostles' next line. Verse 5: "And the apostles said to the Lord, 'increase our faith.'"

Then Jesus gives what seems to be a paradoxical answer.

Verse 6: "So the Lord said, 'If you have faith as a mustard seed, you can say to this mulberry tree, "Be pulled up by the roots and be planted in the sea," and it would obey you.'" He's not talking about great faith is He? How big is a mustard seed? It's so small that if I had one in my hand, you would barely see it. Jesus is saying it doesn't take great faith to do what He says. In fact, if you just have faith the size of a mustard seed, you can speak to the tree, the mulberry, or the sycamine tree. He could be referring to a root of bitterness. If you've allowed unforgiveness to develop into a root of bitterness, it still doesn't take great faith to root that thing out of your heart.

Look at the context in the next verses.

> "And which of you, having a servant [remember the servant analogy in Matthew 18:23–35] plowing or tending sheep, will say to him when he has come in from the field, 'Come at once and sit down to eat'? But will he not rather say to him, 'Prepare something for my supper, and gird yourself and serve me till I have eaten and drunk, and afterward you will eat and drink'?"

Was Jesus telling us that He would tell the servant what a good job he had done and how the master would now wait on the servant? No! Jesus is telling us that after the servant has done what was required, he is still the servant at the end of the day.

> "Does he thank the servant because he did the things that were commanded him? I think not. So likewise you, when you have done all those things which you are commanded [What things? Forgiven him seven times for the same offense when he asks you to forgive him] say,

'We are unprofitable servants. We have done what was our duty to do.'"

In other words, we don't get any special brownie points for merely doing what God commands of us. This is our Christian duty, and we can do it.

Forgiveness Comes with Repentance

Our problem is that we misunderstand what forgiveness is. We think forgiveness is emotional joy. Stop and think; are we glad to see the offender for the eighth time? No. Forgiveness is a commitment that is based on a decision. Because the person who offended me came to me and took responsibility for what he did, then I, by an act of my will, will forgive him. Now, the feelings may take a while to catch up, but they will catch up. However, I don't base it on the feelings; I base it on the commitment.

Let's look at Luke 15, the story of the prodigal son once more. The prodigal son went to his dad, "Dad, give me the inheritance." And off he goes into a far country to waste the entire inheritance on wild turkey, wild women, and whatever else wild he finds to waste his money on. He basically lived the life of the sinner until he ran out of money. But the father didn't send him money when he was away. Dad didn't call him on the phone and say, "Son, how are you doing? I love you, son. Oh, you need money? Coming right up. I'll wire it tomorrow." No. The father did not extend to him the benefit of relationship when he was in the prodigal lifestyle. Then one day the prodigal son is out there feeding the pigs and realizes that this Purina pig chow is better than what he is eating. So he says, "I'm going back to my dad's house and tell him I'll work for him as a servant, because I know that my dad's employees are eating better than I am." So he begins the journey back to his dad's house, and the Bible says his dad saw him far away. The dad was looking for him, but he wasn't going to take care of him where he was. The son had to repent. The son comes back and says, "Dad, I want to be a hired hand." But Dad doesn't even want to know about it. He says, "No. This is my son which was dead . . . get the ring, get the robe, kill the fatted calf." In other words, all debt was discharged. All privilege was restored. Why? Because forgiveness and fellowship were extended when repentance came. The prodigal son did not show up at the father's house with pigs. Forgiveness comes with repentance. These are the two sides to that $100 bill.

Remember the example previously quoted in 2 Corinthians, chapter 2, verses 5–7, concerning a man that was turned away. He was disfellowshipped. We don't know what the sin was; it's not important. The point is that he was turned out of the fellowship.

> But if anyone has caused grief, he has not grieved me, but all of you to some extent—not to be too severe. This punishment [turning him out] which was inflicted by the majority is sufficient for such a man, so that, on the contrary, you ought rather to forgive and comfort him, lest perhaps such a one be swallowed up with too much sorrow.

Sorrow indicates that he has repented. He has taken responsibility for his sin.

> Therefore I urge you to reaffirm your love to him.

Love never stopped. Love is reaffirmed, but forgiveness in this context (the two sides of the $100 bill) is not extended until the man repents.

CHAPTER THREE

THE EVIL PERSON

Paul writes in 1 Corinthians 5:9–13,

> I wrote to you in my epistle not to keep company with sexually immoral people. Yet I certainly did not mean with the sexually immoral people of this world, or with the covetous, or extortioners, or idolaters, since then you would need to go out of the world. [You would have to go live on the moon! You can't be in the world and not be exposed to people of the world.] But now I have written to you not to keep company with anyone named a brother, who is sexually immoral, or covetous, or an idolater, or a reviler, or a drunkard, or an extortioner—not even to eat with such a person.

May I tell you something? We've had crooks in our church before and I had to ask forgiveness from my congregation after studying this, because I did not act as swiftly as I should have. When there is a pattern of behavior where someone is trading on the name of Christ, it's the responsibility of leadership to confront him or her, and if you have ever been swindled by a "brother," it's your responsibility to rebuke him. Would that kind of situation cause somebody to lose their faith? A person gets saved and water baptized and the next thing, they get hooked up with a swindler-brother who takes them to the cleaners. People make shipwreck of their faith over these things. We should not allow that. Unity, as far as God is concerned, is extremely important, and it should also be esteemed by us individually. Unity is not compromise but agreement on truth.

Paul goes on (verse 12): "For what have I to do with judging those also who are outside? Do you not judge those who are inside?" Right now you are probably thinking that the Bible says to judge not lest we be judged, but when you got saved, God didn't say to check your brain at the door!

Verse 13: "But those who are outside [the unbelievers] God judges. Therefore put away from yourselves the evil person." Hmmm. The evil person is a brother, by the way, or at least named a brother. That phrase, "put away from yourselves the evil person" is interesting. In the Old Testament it is used to refer to the false prophet. Guess how the false prophet was put away? It was with the "heave offering." He was stoned to death! In the Old Testament, the phrase also applied to the person who would bring false witness against his brother in order to have him convicted wrongfully. If the false witness was found out, the very punishment of the crime that was to be inflicted on the one he accused was to be put upon him. Remember, the character of God has not changed.

I've been asked what the difference is between murder and killing. Look it up in the dictionary. There is a very clear distinction. The Bible does not prohibit killing under certain circumstances. God told Moses, "Thou shalt not do murder." But if God said we shall not kill, then God violated His own commandment and empowered His people to violate it many times. Obviously, that's not what He said. If you think that bloodshed was extreme in the past, wait until Jesus comes back! God is still the God of justice.

A Two-way Street

Let's put this into practical application. Is the benefit of fellowship restored without repentance? If the offender has not recognized the offense or is not willing to take responsibility for the offense (that is, to repent), can the relationship be restored to original health? I don't believe so. Obviously, we should not be hateful, mean-spirited, or bitter, but neither can we ignore the issue. The passage in Luke 17, which we studied earlier, tells us that if the offender repents, forgive him. We continue to love even if offended, but the vulnerability and the sweetness of relationship is a two-way street. If a brother abuses me and sins against me in this context, I have to extend forgiveness to him from my heart whether he repents or not, but until he repents, I'm not willing to open myself up again and be vulnerable and allow him to continue to abuse me. How far do we go with forgiveness? I believe we should go as far as we can without allowing the abuse to happen again. The line is drawn there, and if the abuse begins to cross it, draw the line back even closer. God has not called us to be abused. Remember, I'm not talking about persecution for righteousness' sake; I'm talking about evil people, even those who call themselves brothers, who abuse us.

For the sake of clarity, let's put aside the term "forgiveness" and just look at the workings of relationship. When offense (a major sin) comes, it must be addressed before the relationship can be restored to healthy status. Even without the offender repenting, the wounded one must not harbor bitterness. I'm not telling you to be unforgiving—the analogy of the $100 bill expresses it very well. In fact, the wounded one is told to love his or her brother without basing that love on behavior. Love continues even with an unrepentant brother.

Another example would be when a transgressor asks for forgiveness in an area such as child molestation or sexual abuse. Forgiveness must be given when repentance is offered. That is not an option. But wisdom would place limits on exposure of my children to that type of individual. Once again, just because you got saved, you didn't lose your brain. "I, wisdom, dwell with prudence . . ." (Proverbs 8:12).

Forgiveness without Repentance

Now let's talk about the other side of this issue that we haven't addressed yet—the side of forgiving without repentance.
Mark 11:22–25:

> So Jesus answered and said to them, "Have faith in God. For assuredly, I say to you, whoever says to this mountain, 'Be removed and be cast into the sea,' and does not doubt in his heart, but believes that those things he says will be done, he will have whatever he says . . ."

Did Jesus really say "whatever?" Did you know this verse was in the Bible? Look at that again: "For assuredly, I say to you . . ."

"When the super-spiritual one says to this mountain . . ." Does it say that? "When the intercessor says . . ." No. "When the pastor says . . ." No. Who? "Whoever." That means you and me. Verse 23 continues:

> "Whoever says to this mountain, 'Be removed and be cast into the sea,' and does not doubt in his heart, but believes that those things he says will be done, he will have whatever he says. Therefore I say to you, whatever things you ask when you pray, believe that you receive them, and you will have them. And whenever you stand praying [here it is], if you have anything against anyone, forgive him [there's the one side of the $100 bill], that your Father in heaven may also forgive you your trespasses . . ."

Extending forgiveness to an unrepentant offender is not easy. Sometimes the offender is malicious and deliberate in attacking you. However, the requirement to forgive remains, and God's grace always gives to us what God requires. We can walk in the steps of our Lord who from the cross cried out, "Father, forgive them for they do not know what they are doing." This was forgiveness extended to unrepentant people and did not imply regeneration.

In your mind, go back to the Lord's Prayer with me. "Our Father in heaven, hallowed be Your name. Your kingdom come. Your will be done on earth as it is in heaven. Give us this day our daily bread. And forgive us our debts as we forgive our debtors . . ." There it is again, the one side of the $100 bill—extending forgiveness. But once again, not extending the fruit of relationship until repentance.

As God's children we have received the enablement to extend forgiveness. Romans 5:5: "the love of God has been poured out within our hearts through the Holy Spirit who was given to us."

Extending forgiveness may seem difficult, but by God's grace we can obey Him and forgive. Here is half of the $100 bill that we are commanded by our Lord to always extend. Not only is forgiveness commanded, it is always in our best interest.

Conclusion

Medical science shows us that unforgiveness and bitterness can damage our health. As God's people, we *always* extend forgiveness, but we must be wise in understanding what that means.

My desire is to grow and mature in Christ, thereby being able to speak the truth in love. Maturity not only speaks the truth, it does so in love. I'm not fully matured yet, but I will press on.

This truth of forgiveness is a vital message in the context of being God's people and the family of believers. Whether you have done this correctly or not in the past is irrelevant. What matters is now.

We can work out our own salvation in fear and trembling because God is at work in us both to will and to do His good pleasure. We can live together in community and display this incredible love that God has already placed in our hearts. We are the people of God; we are His children.

Psalm 138:8 tells us that God will perfect that which concerns us. His mercy endures forever, and we are His workmanship.

Finally, be encouraged in His grace. He is the One who saw you before you were born and loved you. He loves you with an everlasting love; therefore, with His loving-kindness He has drawn you.

> Behold what manner of love the Father has bestowed on us, that we should be called children of God!
>
> (1 John 3:1)

EPILOGUE
BY JOHN SAMSON

For those of you who have read thus far, I would like to introduce John Samson. I have known John for over twenty years, and in my opinion, he is one of the finest teachers in the body of Christ. I have asked John to contribute his thoughts in this epilogue and I am confident you will be blessed.

(Pastor Bruce Brock)

The truths you have read so far are vital and essential in human relationship. Human relationships have been examined in the clear light of Scripture; problem areas have been uncovered and important questions have been answered. I believe many will be able to say God has given them the help and direction they need in these pages.

I would like you to see repentance from yet another perspective—a heavenly perspective. If we can see something of this, it will greatly increase our gratitude for its operation in our lives.

Born from Above

In the early verses of John chapter 3, Jesus tells Nicodemus in no uncertain terms the absolute necessity of being born again or, "*born from above.*" Unless a man is first born again, or regenerated, he can never enter or even see the kingdom of God. Jesus stresses the fact that this new birth is not merely an optional extra. It is imperative. Jesus said in John 3:7, "You must be born again."

Jesus didn't tell Nicodemus what he must do to be born again. That is because it was not within Nicodemus' power to perform this miracle. "That which is born of the flesh is flesh, and that which is born of the Spirit is spirit" (John 3:6). Flesh can only reproduce flesh. It takes the Spirit to regenerate the human spirit. This miracle of regeneration cannot be achieved by human effort.

The new birth is not the improvement of the old nature but the creation of an entirely new one. It is a birth, a new birth, and like the first one we experienced, it did not occur because of our decision to be born. We were born as a result of the will of others—that of our parents, and of course, God's will to create us using the means of human, physical intimacy. In contrast to our first birth, this spiritual new birth does not occur through human means. God alone brings about this new creation in Christ Jesus. As John 1:12–13 points out:

> But as many as received Him, to them He gave the right to become children of God, to those who believe in His name: who were born, not of blood, nor of the will of the flesh, nor of the will of man, but of God.

Human flesh can only reproduce flesh. It is the Holy Spirit alone who can recreate human spirits. The Holy Spirit is the sole Agent working regeneration in the human spirit.

This Is All Very Mysterious

In explaining this phenomenon of the new birth, Jesus speaks of something very mysterious—the wind. Wind is mysterious because it is something we've never actually seen. We know it is around because of its effects, but we've never actually observed wind with our eyes. We've seen trees swaying, leaves falling, and papers flying through the air. Sometimes the effect of the wind is so powerful that the only word we can use would be "devastation." Wind can cause havoc on a massive scale, as victims of a hurricane can testify. Wind is mysterious because we cannot see it. We are never sure about where it came from or where it is going. It seems to have a mind of its own.

Concerning this, Jesus said in John 3:8, "The wind blows where it wishes, and you hear the sound of it, but cannot tell where it comes from and where it goes. So it is with everyone who is born of the Spirit."

The word *pneuma* in Greek, like the word *ruach* in Hebrew, means "breath, wind, or spirit." Jesus uses an obvious play on words here, describing the activity of the Holy Spirit in regeneration.

Much more could be said about these opening verses in John chapter 3, but I want to stop and appreciate the impact of verse 8. Here, Jesus teaches us that when anyone is born of the Spirit, like the blowing of the wind, the invisible, sovereign, Spirit of God has moved in mighty power. Yet in contrast to when a town or city experiences storm damage on a large scale, the effect of this "wind" is not in any way negative. Though powerful in the extreme, the Holy Spirit's work is amazingly positive and precise.

When someone is born again, it is evidence of the fact that God, the Holy Spirit, has performed extensive divine surgery. He has taken out the stony heart and put in a heart of flesh. Using the biblical imagery of Ezekiel, flesh is spoken of in contrast to stone, as Ezekiel 36:26–27 declares,

> I will give you a new heart and put a new spirit within you; I will take the heart of stone out of your flesh and give you a heart of flesh. I will put my Spirit within you and cause you to walk in My statutes, and you will keep My judgments and do them.

I remember going to a Christian service at age fourteen. I was only there because my father had asked me to go. I had no interest in Christ, and I certainly had no interest in what the preacher had to say. But sometime during the message, my attitude changed. I became interested. In fact, I became intrigued. I was fascinated and struck by the realities of heaven and hell and the need for a Savior. For the first time in my life, I was attracted by a treasure I had never seen before.

I know now that what happened was God, the Holy Spirit. While I was hearing the gospel, God went to work on my soul. In an instant in time, I was born from above, the old heart of stone was removed and a new heart was put in, and with every beat I wanted to know the Master, our Lord Jesus Christ. Jesus stepped off the old dusty pages of the Bible and became a living person in my eyes. All of a sudden, I really wanted to know Him. I wanted Him to save me, and I wanted His will in my life. When the gospel appeal was made, I came to Christ willingly in repentance and faith.

If you are born of the Spirit, God did the exact same thing for you. It is God and God alone who has saved us. All the credit belongs to Him, because this birth had nothing to do with our intelligence (that we somehow worked out who Jesus was for ourselves) or our humility (we were able to humble ourselves to respond in repentance and faith to the gospel). We are Christians because of the all-conquering power of the mighty Spirit of God, who graciously stormed our hearts and worked His sovereign will. He brought us forth by the word of truth, causing us to find sheer delight in the presence of God both now and for all eternity.

When Lazarus was raised from death, everyone marveled at the all-powerful call of Jesus. By the power of just His word, He actually brought a corpse back to life. Of course, no one was more thrilled with this divine mercy than Lazarus himself.

Why am I emphasizing God's grace in this way? Because with Lazarus we can say that by the effectual call of God, grace has conquered our hearts and brought us to life when we were spiritually dead in our trespasses and sins. The Greek word for dead in Ephesians 2:1 means "dead like a corpse," but God made us alive (Ephesians 2:5).

The apostle Paul wrote the following in Ephesians 2:1–5:

> And you He made alive, who were dead in trespasses and sins, in which you once walked according to the course of this world, according to the prince of the power of the air, the spirit who now works in the sons of disobedience, among whom also we all once conducted ourselves in the lusts of our flesh, fulfilling the desires of the flesh and of the mind, and were by nature children of wrath, just as the others. But God, who is rich in mercy, because of His great love with which He loved us, even when we were dead in trespasses, made us alive together with Christ (by grace you have been saved) . . .

Scripture is clear that man, left to himself, is totally incapable of coming to Christ. Jesus said in John 6:44, "No one can come to Me unless the Father who sent Me draws him; and I will raise him up at the last day." He repeated the exact same idea later in verse 65 when He said, "no one can come to Me unless it has been granted him by My Father."

You might ask, "Doesn't the Bible command us to repent of our sins and turn to Christ?" Yes, it does, and here are two Scripture verses in Mark 1:14–15 that affirm this:

> Now after John was put in prison, Jesus came to Galilee, preaching the gospel of the kingdom of God, and saying, "The time is fulfilled, and the kingdom of God is at hand. Repent, and believe in the gospel."

And Luke 13:3:

> ". . . unless you repent you will all likewise perish."

You might think, "If God commands us to do something, doesn't that mean that we must have the ability to do what He commands? It would not seem just for God to command us to do what we are incapable of doing." At first glance, this does seem to be a legitimate and logical idea. If God demands something of us, then surely we must have the ability to do it.

But not so fast! If we stop and think about it for a moment, there are a number of commands God makes of the human race that we are powerless to do in and of ourselves. It doesn't take long to realize that even with the first of the Ten Commandments—loving God with all our heart, soul, mind and strength—God is commanding something of us that we have failed to do for even one twenty-four-hour period in our lives. Can you and I honestly say that we have loved God with our whole heart today or that all of our thoughts today have been pleasing to Him? No, we can't.

God very clearly commands us to be perfect and to be holy. That would be hard enough, even if we were to make up our own human standard of perfection or holiness. The divine command leaves no wiggle room to set the bar at a level we can attain. Jesus said in Matthew 5:48, "be perfect, just as your Father in heaven is perfect." We are commanded to live at the same level of perfection that God does. The same is true concerning God's holiness. In 1 Peter 1:16, God says, "Be holy, for I am holy."

God is within His rights to ask this of us, but the fact is: although we are entirely responsible to do this, it is totally impossible for us to do in and of ourselves. This is not because we have some mental or physical handicap but because while we are alive our sinful nature is all too present with us and it is bent toward sin. Since Adam's sin plunged the human race into corruption, we are not so much sinners because we sin, but we sin because we are sinners.

Jesus invites or commands us, "Come to Me, all you who labor and are heavy laden, and I will give you rest" (Matthew 11:28). Yet, as we saw in John 6:44, Scripture teaches us that we are unable to come to Him: "No one can come to Me . . ." We are unable to come to Christ unless God in His grace does something to intervene: "unless the Father who sent Me draws him; and I will raise him up at the last day."

God commands us to, "Seek the LORD while He may be found, call upon Him while He is near" (Isaiah 55:6). Yet, Scripture clearly teaches in Romans 3:11: "There is none who understands; there is none who seeks after God." And it will always be this way, unless God graciously intervenes, as it states in Romans 10:20: "I was found by those who did not seek Me; I was made manifest to those who did not ask for Me."

Now, let's look at the matter of the human heart. God tells Israel, "get yourselves a new heart and a new spirit. For why should you die, O house of Israel?" (Ezekiel 18:31).

But again, here's the problem: "The heart is deceitful above all things, and desperately wicked . . ." (Jeremiah 17:9).

So what is the remedy? The answer, once again, is found in God's mercy and grace: "I will give you a new heart and put a new spirit within you; and I will take the heart of stone out of your flesh and give you a heart of flesh" (Ezekiel 36:26).

Repentance and Faith

It is clear from even a casual glance through Scripture that God commands all people to repent and believe the gospel. If we fail to do this, we perish.

Repentance and faith brings full justification and fellowship in the sight of God. We are justified by a repenting kind of faith. This faith renounces self-effort to gain acceptance with God and, turning from sin, loves Christ and trusts in Christ alone to save. That is the nature of true genuine faith. It is a repenting kind of faith—and an enduring faith. Repentance and faith are our acts; they are something we do. Yet, these acts of repentance and faith are the result of God's activity in our heart.

Repentance Is a Gift

We have a responsibility of proclaiming the good news of Christ's gospel, but we must recognize the fact that it is God who opens up people's hearts (Acts 16:14). We are called to proclaim Christ's message, but at the same time, we must relate to others in a gracious way when we do this.

To do this in a Christ-like manner, 2 Timothy 2:24–26 tells us,

> And a servant of the Lord must not quarrel but
> be gentle to all, able to teach, patient, in hu-
> mility correcting those who are in opposition,
> if God perhaps will grant them repentance, so
> that they may know the truth, and that they
> may come to their senses and escape the snare
> of the devil, having been taken captive by him
> to do his will.

We don't know who the elect, or "born again," are. They are not walking around the countryside with the letter E for Elect stamped upon their forehead. We are told to go into all the world and preach the gospel to everyone. We are to show kindness, patience, and gentleness, even when we correct those who oppose the truth, knowing ahead of time that only God's elect will respond in genuine repentance and faith. From all eternity, God has assigned us the role of being His spokesperson when He imparts the gift of repentance to a person. This is an amazing privilege and awesome responsibility we have.

Faith Is a Gift

"Not all have faith," as 2 Thessalonians 3:2 declares, but those who do have been given a gift. This fact is confirmed when we read that faith was something given or "granted" to the Christians at Philippi: "For to you it has been *granted on behalf of Christ,* not only *to believe in Him,* but also to suffer for His sake . . ." (Philippians 1:29). As we read this verse, notice that believing in Christ is something granted to us. It is a gracious gift, and what is true for the Christians in Philippi is true concerning Christians everywhere.

"Now when the Gentiles heard this [the presentation of the gospel], they were glad and glorified the word of the Lord. And as many as had been appointed to eternal life believed"

(Acts 13:48). The gospel was presented to them, and all who had the appointment, made the appointment. All those who were appointed to eternal life believed the gospel when they heard it.

"And when he [Apollos] arrived, he greatly helped those who had believed through grace" (Acts 18:27). Faith is not the product of our human nature, but is in fact, a gift, and "Jesus is the author and finisher of our faith" (Hebrews 12:2).

What Exactly Is the Gift?

In Ephesians 2:8–9 we read,

> For by grace you have been saved through faith,
> and that not of yourselves; it is the gift of God,
> not of works, lest anyone should boast.

In verse 8, what exactly does the "that" refer to? Can we pinpoint what is not of ourselves but is the gift of God? This is vitally important to our entire understanding of salvation. Is it the "grace," the "salvation," or the "faith" that is the gift of God?

The answer is *all of the above.* The grace, the salvation, and even the faith—*all these things* are the gift of God.

This emphasis in Scripture is something the Holy Spirit has revealed to us not for the sake of boasting. Once revealed to us, man's pride is humbled and brought low as God's grace is exalted, magnified, and put on display. We are to be amazed and astounded by the depth and power of God's grace that brings a sinner to repentance and faith. In the midst of our trials and struggles, God wants us to find comfort and edification in the fact that our choice of Him stems first from His choice of us.

Christ's chosen sheep will hear His voice. That is our only hope in proclaiming the gospel message. In John 10, verse 16,

Jesus said, "and other sheep I have which are not of this fold; them also I must bring, and they will hear My voice; and there will be one flock and one shepherd."

We must preach the gospel; we must declare it in clear terms. We must also recognize that even if we possessed the skill of an expert preacher, it is not in our power to make anyone see the beauty in the gospel. Our hope is that as we preach God will open the eyes of people and shine His light into their hearts in such a way that for the very first time they can see the glory and the beauty of Christ.

God's saving purposes cannot be thwarted—none of Christ's true sheep will ever be lost (John 6:37–39, 10:26–30). This salvation involves the work of the Trinity. All who are chosen by God the Father, redeemed by Christ the Son, and given faith by the Holy Spirit, are eternally saved. They are kept in faith by the power of God and thus persevere to the end. They persevere in faith because He preserves them.

The gospel is not merely something non-Christians desperately need but something every Christian needs to hear repeatedly. We need to preach the gospel to ourselves every day, for it lies at the very center of the Christian life. Applying the gospel to every area of our life is also the way to experience God's intended victory and blessing. God saves sinners, and salvation is of the Lord!